MOTIVATE THIS!

How to Start Each Day with an **UNSTOPPABLE ATTITUDE TO SUCCEED REGARDLESS** of Your Circumstances

STEVE RIZZO

PEARHOUSE PRESS
.COM

Published by Pearhouse Press, Pittsburgh, Pennsylvania
pearhousepress.com

Cover and Book Design: Mike Murray

Printed in the United States of America.

ISBN: 978-0-9886721-7-8
LCCN: 2016951087

This book is dedicated to my friends and colleagues who, in their own way, were the Spark that Ignited Change in my Life.

Table of Contents

Introduction ■ 3

1
The Challenge with Motivation ■ 9

2
It's All About How You Feel ■ 15

3
The Wrath of Self-Curse-Talk ■ 23

4
Enjoyment: A Shift into High Gear ■ 33

5
The Greatest Motivator of All ■ 41

6
Motivation + Life Balance = Happiness ■ 47

7
Shift Your Motivation & Honor Your Values ■ 55

8
Start Each Day with an Unstoppable Attitude! ■ 65

INTRODUCTION

How Motivated Are You?

EACH ONE OF YOU READING THIS BOOK will have a different perspective on what motivation is, how it is defined and how that definition relates to you. But everyone reading this book will improve his or her overall degree of motivation on all levels of life as a result of it.

Here are some questions for you to ponder in that brain of yours. What is your personal truth? Are you grateful for what you have, or are you resentful and bitter about what is lacking? Do you feel blessed? Cursed? Do you learn from your mistakes and move forward with confidence, or do you berate yourself and quit for fear of failing? Do you believe you're worthy enough of success and happiness, or do you believe dreams are for more fortunate people? Are you the victor or the victim? Do you savor and enjoy the moment, or do you live by the clock and believe you just don't have time to laugh and enjoy the process?

Right now you're probably wondering, "Why all the questions?" Well...I have absolutely no idea! Of course, I'm joking. Trust me—I'm in control here. Perhaps I should have introduced myself first. I guess this is as good a time as any. Hi! I'm Steve Rizzo, comedian-turned-motivator. Welcome to *Motivate THIS*.

Now, where was I…Oh yeah…I remember: How you answer all of the above questions creates the beliefs that shape how you experience your life. Your beliefs write your story. Stop and ask yourself, *Am I writing a story of abundance and joy? Or am I writing a story of scarcity and despair?* It is sad indeed to watch naturally gifted people who have every advantage and possibility of success strip themselves of empowerment because they lack the motivation to forge ahead. Bad habits and years of negative reinforcement create a belief system that convinces them they are not good enough, worthy enough, smart enough, fortunate enough and a host of other "not enoughs" that cause them to foil their own dreams and sabotage their own success and happiness.

Here's my point, dear reader. I want to make this very clear:

Nothing stifles motivation more than a toxic belief system. *Nothing!*

On the other hand, nothing fuels motivation more than a positive belief system. I will explain in detail how this process works later. For now, here's the CliffsNotes version:

Your beliefs, positive and negative, are formed over a period of time through a consistent way of thinking. In other words, your thoughts create your beliefs. You got that? Good. Your beliefs cause you to feel a certain way. The feelings you have on any given day, good or bad, dictate the tone of your attitude. The attitude you have on any given day regulates your overall degree of motivation. This entire process eventually leads to the choices you make and the actions you take.

In 1992, I was sitting backstage at the Sands Hotel in Atlantic City. I had just finished the rehearsal for my SHOWTIME comedy special that was to take place the following night. Woody Harrelson, who was hosting the show, approached me and asked me how I wanted to be introduced. I thought for a moment and said, *"Tell them that you're going to bring in someone who was voted 'Least Likely to Succeed' in high school. Now he's here in Atlantic City at the Sands Hotel filming a SHOWTIME special!"* Yes, I was one of a number of students voted "Least Likely to Succeed." Although the names on that list never made it into the yearbook, and at the time I took it as a big joke, the damage was still done.

Now I understand that it was that type of negative labeling that branded me and influenced the direction my life took. It instilled so much fear in me that it stifled motivation and impeded my ability to move forward. My philosophy was, *"If you don't try, you can't fail."* (Talk about lack of motivation!) This was the only way I knew how to avoid the rejection and failure I was convinced would result from anything I did. So...I turned my back on many opportunities. Even when I did push forward to make the effort, all it took was just one misstep or one criticism from someone in authority to reinforce the belief that I wasn't good enough.

These internal labels are created by the beliefs we have about ourselves and our surrounding world. They begin to formulate when we are children and, for the most part, are bestowed upon us by our parents, teachers, religious groups and peers.

Of course, we want to give the adults in our lives the benefit of the doubt and assume their intentions were good; nonetheless, the results may have been devastating. Children are vulnerable to the opinions and thoughts of others. Some labels are programmed into a young mind by a dominating parent who never gave the child a chance to think for herself. *"I know what's best for you...You listen to me." "I know what will make you happy."* Others may have been told by a teacher or some other authority figure that they simply weren't smart enough or good enough to fulfill their dream. *"I don't think you're cut out for this. Why don't you try something else?"*

Whatever messages you received when you were young became your reality and the labels you wore into adulthood. Unknowingly, we take them to the workplace and wear them in our personal lives. You might be wearing a positive label that signifies that you are smart and have the confidence to meet any challenge head on. If so, that is the brand you carry everywhere you go. You might be wearing a toxic label that signifies you are not good enough and are incapable of making wise decisions. That, too, is your brand, and it will influence every decision you make. Either way, labels represent who you *think* you are. Your labels, good or bad, determine the choices you make and the actions you take.

Whether positive or negative, your labels are the foundation of your life. Why? Because they set the tone for how motivated you are from day to day. Your success and happiness are built upon them. If your foundation is comprised of fear, anger, self-doubt, hopelessness and being overwhelmed, the label you wear is toxic. Nothing can distort the way you view your life and your surrounding world worse. They have the power to paralyze you physically, mentally, emotionally and spiritually.

The labels you've placed on yourself have an impact on how you react to the day-to-day circumstances that make up your daily life. And, as a result, that reality then becomes your story. The more you hold on to the stories created by the negative labels you wear, the more you validate the false reality they represent and the less motivated you become. This continuing cycle has a profound effect on your destiny.

That said, it's important to understand that your personal circumstances are made up of the string of events that occur in your life. It's what you do or how you choose to respond to these events that determines how your story is written. Once you seize control and challenge the negative labels you carry, your life circumstances begin to shift in a healthier, more productive direction. So does your momentum to become, and stay, motivated.

Toxic beliefs do not have to write your story. Why? Because you are the author. You get to decide how it will be written when you choose to experience the events in your life in a certain way. The good news is that you can choose to experience these events from an *advantage* point of view.

This book offers insights as to what stifles motivation, lessons on how to create a better you and Common Sense Success Strategies on how to start each day with an unstoppable attitude to succeed, how to keep the motivation going throughout the day, every day, regardless of your circumstances. I know this is a bold statement to make, but these strategies are what I used to turn my life around. I honestly believe that if I can do it, so can you.

Right now you might be thinking, "Oh, come on, Steve-O! Are you telling me that all I have to do is use your Common Sense Success Strategies and I can stay motivated throughout the day no matter what madness is going on in my life?"

Of course, it will be easier for some than others, but, yes, that's exactly what I'm saying. The goal is not to just read or memorize these strategies, but to make them a habit. That's your job and your responsibility. When you allow these strategies to become a part of who you are, a gradual transformation will begin to take place. You will notice a shift in attitude and you will actually feel good about yourself and your surrounding world. A State of Feeling Good is not only a key to success, but also a crucial element to motivation and a major theme throughout my book.

We allow situations, circumstances and people to suck the energy right out of us because we don't know we have the power to transform our lives. Well…guess what? You *do* have that power! And the information in this book can unleash it.

Is this a business book? YES! It will give you insights and examples that you can apply to coworkers and customers.

Is this a personal book? Yes! It will give you insights and examples on how to stay motivated to achieve your personal goals and everyday tasks.

Is this a life book? YES! It will give you insights and examples that you can apply to yourself. It will bring you from down to up. It will bring you from woe is me to WOW is me!

One more thing, dear reader. Have fun reading this book and allow yourself to embrace the simple message that it conveys. If you do, you will discover increased productivity, greater enthusiasm, new levels of success and a higher degree of happiness. What you are about to read transformed my life for the better when I didn't think such an outcome was possible or within my power to achieve. I am happy to share it. ■

1

The Challenge
with Motivation

ONE OF THE BIGGEST CHALLENGES WE FACE TODAY is keeping ourselves motivated to be at our best. I believe the challenge lies not just in knowing how to get motivated, but how to stay motivated and optimistic for more than just a few days.

Most companies put a great deal of time and energy into hiring people they believe are qualified to fill a particular position. But there is no guarantee that even a highly qualified person will always be motivated to be at their best. It simply means they have what it takes to get the job done.

Some companies spend a lot of time and money to make sure that everyone is equipped with the right tools and resources to get the job done. Some employers give incentives in the way of promotions, raises and bonuses in the hope that their employees will excel in their chosen field of expertise. Others go to great lengths to educate their employees by having them attend seminars and training courses with the expectation that they will walk away with tools, confidence and a desire to be their best self.

All of the above are important criteria for success. But, do they truly motivate? If so (and, most importantly), how long does the motivation last? It's easy to stay motivated for a few days or when everything is going as planned. Who can stay motivated for the long haul, though, especially when times are tough and the pressure is on? This brings me to my next point.

Whether they realize it or not, employees bring their situations, experiences, personal challenges and problems from home to the workplace. Yet there has always been a preconceived notion that we are supposed to have the capacity to separate our personal lives from our professional lives.

What this really implies is that if you are having problems in your personal life, regardless of the severity, you should have the mental and emotional fortitude to put those problems aside while you are at work. Yeah, right! This is an expectation that is easier said than done. Let me explain.

Both your personal and professional lives are parts of you that make up your whole being. No matter where you go or what you are doing, the other part of you will always be tagging along assuring you that everything's alright or forever haunting you that something is not right somewhere in your world.

Let's say you're going through a divorce, or you're having financial difficulties. Maybe you're dealing with health issues, or there's an illness in the family. Perhaps you are experiencing the death of a loved one. Stuff happens. It's very difficult, if not impossible, not to take these types of problems and concerns with you to the workplace every morning. And, unless you have the tools and strategies that can help you to embrace life's unfortunate circumstances, they will have some kind of effect on how you do your job. It's only natural.

The point I'm making here is that it's hard to be at your very best at work if your personal life is under intense stress. Our personal problems and the moods, attitudes and feelings that follow have to be weighed in as factors as to how motivated we are at work. Likewise, if you are experiencing tough times at work, it's difficult not to take those concerns home with you, and there is a good chance that it will have some kind of negative impact on your personal life. Some people get caught up in this vicious cycle day in and day out.

It's hard to be at your very best at work if your personal life is under intense stress.

There are other outside factors that stifle motivation that need to be taken into consideration as well. Let's call them environmental and social stressors. They affect almost everyone in one way or another. Some days are worse than others.

I think we can all agree that we're living in a world that's moving incredibly fast. Today, we have many high-tech advantages at our disposal to make our lives so much easier, yet we seem to be more stressed out than ever before. Remember the saying "Patience is a virtue?" Well, it's pretty much lost its meaning.

It seems like we have created a mindset at work and in our lives where everyone wants what they want when they want it. If we don't get it when we want it or the way we want it, we feel ripped off. There are people that hold on to their bad moods and negative attitudes all day simply because they were stuck in traffic or had to wait too long in line at Starbucks for their *Triple Shot, Skinny, Mocha, Carmel, Blah Blah Blah Whatever You Call It Latte!* Yeah, that's what they need. More caffeine! Give me a break! Better yet, give yourself a break and let it go!

On top of our professional and personal problems and everyday pressures—most of which we put on ourselves—the newspapers and evening newscasts tell us that our economy is falling apart, corporations are being forced to downsize and massive technological advances are causing people to re-evaluate, adjust and change their lives. Cell phones, Blackberries, iPhones and tablet devices, e-mails, text messages and even micro-communication applications like Twitter are clogging our minds with an overwhelming amount of information, leaving us with little or no time to relax, unwind and focus our attention on the big picture.

To compound this, political unrest, crime, disease, prejudice and violence are running rampant just as they have for centuries past. Hold on a second. I need to take a break here. I'm getting depressed. I'll be right back.

[Steve makes a Starbucks run...]

Okay, I'm back now. Where was I? Oh yeah, I remember. The divorce rate is at an all-time high; despite an unwilling public, war seems to be the number one strategy for dealing with conflict between nations; and at any moment we could be the target of a terrorist attack.

It's obvious I'm having fun here, but seriously, all of the above are circumstances that can make us feel off-balance and stifle motivation. They can cripple even the very best from moving forward with optimism. It's really no wonder why so many of us have to be medicated in some way or another in order to cope with the madness our civilizations have created.

The real concern here is that most of us aren't even aware of what's happening to us. We have no idea why we're always stressed out, exhausted and show little enthusiasm. As my father always said, "You can't fix something if you don't know it's broken." Even If we were aware that something was wrong, few of us would know what to do to turn it around.

Have no need to fear! The answers are here! What you are about to experience from this point on is not Brain Surgery. It's more like Brain Adjustment. Throughout the remainder of this book I will be offering ideas, insights, lessons and, as I mentioned earlier, Common Sense Success Strategies that will not only take you to a better place in business, but in life. In my view, that's the ultimate success. ■

2

It's All About
How You Feel

RIGHT NOW, I'M ABOUT TO GIVE YOU A GOLDEN NUGGET of information that can change your life forever. Are you ready? Here it is. The key to starting your day with an unstoppable attitude to succeed—and to keep the motivation going throughout the day—is to make sure you are feeling good during the process of whatever you are trying to achieve. That's it! That's all you need to know. You can now close the book and go about your business, for you are now enlightened. I'm joking, of course. But as simple as this may seem, it truly is the key to staying motivated and achieving the quality of success that you desire. Why? Because feeling good is the fuel that drives motivation. Write that down and slap in on your refrigerator. Here it is again. Say it out loud. Feeling good is the fuel that drives motivation. That's your choice and your responsibility.

Nothing, absolutely nothing, keeps people from staying motivated and achieving their goals more than harboring negative emotions or having a bad attitude during the process. The number one reason people in business fail or have difficulty achieving their goals is because positive momentum ceases. And the reason positive momentum ceases is because the individual is focusing all of their energy on what isn't working and all of the things that need to be done in order to make it work. This type of chaotic thinking leaves the individual with no room at all in that brain of theirs for positive thoughts to seep through so they can come up with healthier alternatives or to deal with the next challenge that will inevitably follow moments later. In other words, your life or your business will not work if you keep thinking about what's wrong or what isn't working.

When you are setting out to achieve any goal, you have to be vigilant about what you're focusing on and what you're thinking about. Nothing brings out the *worst* in any negative situation faster than you focusing on it. On the other hand, nothing brings out the *best* in any positive situation faster than you focusing on it. The point is that you have to be aware of what you're focusing on if you want to stay motivated and succeed. Observing a problem only perpetuates it. Trying to figure out how it got started doesn't help. Taking action while feeling negative emotions only compounds the problem. Remember, it isn't necessarily the details of a particular challenge that weigh us down, but our own self-induced negative energy that keeps us from thinking positive and moving forward with hope and optimism.

It simply makes sense that a situation will only improve once you improve the way you feel. Finding relief and making yourself feel good is crucial and needs to be the very first step toward turning any stressful, challenging or negative situation around.

Nothing brings out the *worst* in any negative situation faster than you focusing on it.

A State of Feeling Good is the foundation on which everyone should build their business and life. As you well know, when you're in the process of building the business or life that you desire, things will not always go the way you want. You will no doubt face challenges, obstacles and even fear along the way. Sometimes your plans will fall apart. The good news is that you can always rebuild on a rock solid foundation. A State of Feeling Good will give you that foundation over and over again.

As a child, I acquired many fears and limiting beliefs about myself and the world that surrounded me. For a great part of my life I believed circumstances determined my fate. I didn't understand that I could have chosen a better way. My experiences with adults, teachers and my peers led me to believe that I simply wasn't good enough or smart enough. After being saddled with the dubious high school honor of "Least Likely to Succeed," and after being told by a guidance counselor that I didn't have the intelligence to make it through college, I wore the Loser label with a certain amount of twisted pride.

But years of feeling inadequate and habitual negative thinking eventually created labels that led me to believe that dreams were the luxury of only a fortunate few and I wasn't one of them. I woke up every morning waiting for my life to happen. If anyone needed an attitude adjustment, it was me.

The real danger set in when I left home and tried to make it on my own. Looking back, I can see how and why I sabotaged so many opportunities. Unaware, I carried with me many of my unresolved negative labels and limiting beliefs. As a result, I kept reliving the same mistakes and failures over and over again. I knew I had the talent, but I couldn't understand why I wasn't getting my big break. My perceived limitations had me confused, and my fears paralyzed me. In fact, I figured out that I had a fear of failure AND a fear of success. (Talk about not being able to make up your mind.) Sounds crazy, but I never said I was normal.

At the time, I didn't know that fear of failure and success were normal feelings experienced by almost everyone at one time or another. I didn't know I had options on how to respond to those feelings, or that I could have created a healthier belief system simply by consistently shifting my focus and way of thinking. I honestly was clueless to what I know now—you empower yourself when you feel the fear and move forward anyway. Finally, however, I realized that opportunity had been knocking all along. I was just afraid to open the door. I was allowing the toxic labels that had been thrust upon me to dictate the story of my life.

The way that you feel in any given moment is dependent upon and evoked by what you are thinking or saying out loud in any given moment.

Here's my point, dear reader. When I made the decision to make feeling good my number one priority every day, I became aware of a whole new world of possibilities, and the story of my life started to change for the better. I realized that fear, anger, self-doubt or any other negative emotion did not have to set the tone of my attitude if I didn't want them to. Healthier choices instantly presented themselves. I learned how to make myself feel better even when times were tough just by shifting my thoughts and focusing on something that would

3

The Wrath of Self-Curse-Talk

BEFORE WE GO ANY FURTHER, LET'S RECAP what you've already learned. I know this might seem a bit repetitious, but I really want you to get this. Plus, it's my book and I'll do what I want.

So, the key to staying motivated and achieving any goal is to make sure that you are feeling good during the process, even when the situation does not evoke it from you. In other words, whenever you recognize or become aware that you are feeling negative emotions—no matter why, no matter how it got there, no matter what the situation—that is your cue to stop whatever you're doing and gradually shift your focus and thoughts on something that makes you feel better and better and better.

It just makes sense that in order to stay motivated and create positive change when times are tough means to disregard how things

23

are, or how you perceive them to be, and focus your attention on the way you prefer things to be.

Here's how it works: I'm going to create a scenario that will require you to use your imagination. Let's say Charlie works for a major corporate company and, after ten years, the company is taken over by another company. Charlie is promoted and gets a significant raise. After a meeting with the new powers that be, Charlie learns that not only has his job description changed, but now he has a bigger responsibility and he's asked to travel more than usual. So, Charlie does all of the research, goes to all of the meetings and gathers all the information he needs to make his new goals attainable. He is honestly hopeful and confident that things will work out.

Then, somewhere along the way, Charlie encounters some unexpected obstacles, and things don't look as promising as they did when he started. To make matters worse, the workload is piling on and he's away from home more than he wants to be. Soon his enthusiasm turns to frustration, and this frustration turns into self-doubt, worry, anger and fear. It's not long before Charlie's daily inner dialogue morphs into something like this:

"This is absolutely ridiculous. I knew this wasn't going to work. What in the world was I thinking? I must have been out of my mind to think I could do this. I just don't have what it takes. And another thing…No matter what I do or how hard I try, I just don't get the appreciation I deserve! But when someone needs something, whom do they go to? Me, that's who. When I first got this job I was hired to do one thing and one thing only. Now, I'm doing two, three, four, five things at once. What, do I have Victim on my forehead?! To top it all off, they want me to speak at the next meeting. Are they kidding me?! I can't speak in front of groups! Why did they ask me? I'll get all tense and blow it. This is absolutely insane!"

It sure is. I don't know about you, dear reader, but I'm exhausted just writing this.

This entire conditioning process is known by many as negative self-talk. I call it "self-curse-talk" because this type of internal dialogue literally curses you with its power to cast a spell on your life.

Nothing can kill motivation and stifle your attitude to succeed more that self-curse-talk.

The sad truth is that many people who think and talk like this are clueless as to the impact this kind of dialogue has on their quality of life. They have no idea that by allowing negative thoughts to become the majority, they are opening the way for more feelings of hopelessness and defeat. Those very thoughts are creating or reinforcing existing subconscious beliefs that are keeping them from what they desire. They just don't understand that *what they think is what they get* and *what they say out loud is what they ask for*. Likewise, they don't understand why they can't stay motivated.

If there is anything that can keep you from being productive and partaking in the abundance that life has to offer, it's self-curse-talk. If you have a tendency to believe that a tough situation is worse than what it is, it's self-curse-talk. If you're wondering why you're not enjoying the journey of your life, it's self-curse-talk. And if you find yourself more often in a state of unhappiness rather than happiness, it could very well be because of chronic self-curse-talk. In short, nothing can kill motivation and stifle your attitude to succeed more that self-curse-talk.

The thing to understand about self-curse-talk is that it reflects your internalized negative feelings about yourself rather than an empirical truth. In other words, just because you feel it doesn't make it true. Just because you say it to yourself does not make it true. But if you believe that it is true, that's all that matters in your world. That brain of yours (or your subconscious) does not know the difference between true and false. It cannot make independent judgment and instead understands your thoughts to be what they are—just thoughts. If you do not recognize and squash a negative thought when it pops up, your subconscious takes it as truth, thus compounding and affirming that negative feeling and further solidifying a belief system that will have negative consequences.

Allowing one negative thought to go unchallenged first thing in the morning can cause a snowball effect that influences everything you do throughout the day. One negative thought can take an otherwise promising situation and blow it to pieces. Isn't it amazing how no outside help is necessary to ruin your life?

Years ago, my wife and I were in the process of purchasing a house that was built in 1916. We knew at first glance that this was the house of our dreams. It had everything we always wanted in a house. We also knew that a lot of work needed to be done, but still we were both very excited and enthusiastic about our new venture. In fact, we thought that fixing it up would be part of the fun.

One morning, however, I woke up feeling very disturbed and unsure about all of the work that needed to be done. Without realizing what was happening, I was heading straight into the Negative Zone and the culprit was self-curse-talk. *"Did I choose the right contractor? Should I knock out all of the plaster walls and replace them with sheetrock? Should I put the sheetrock over the plaster? If I don't gut the walls I will never know what kind of wiring, plumbing or insulation it has. This could be a fire hazard! Can I really trust this contractor? How do I know I was quoted a fair price? I can't believe I bought this house! I should have purchased a new one! This could wind up being the worst decision I've ever made!"*

Do you see what I was doing to myself? That particular morning I was very close to turning my dream house into the house of horrors. And it all started with one thought. That one thought created a pattern of similar thoughts that eventually caused a negative emotional response. That negative emotional response was setting off unhealthy physiological side effects. My heart was racing, my stomach was tight, and I just didn't feel right. Those physiological side effects were causing me to think more negative thoughts, which, in turn, were causing me to feel more emotionally upset, and so on. To make matters worse, unknowingly, I was taking that emotional baggage to my place of business, and it was interfering with important decisions that needed to be made. It's a vicious cycle that can lead to disastrous results.

Fortunately, I eventually became aware of what I was doing to myself. If I continued reviewing those negative scenarios over and over in my head, I could have convinced myself that the entire project was going to be more trouble than it was worth.

That's what self-curse-talk does. It distorts your reality. It actually leads you to believe that something in your life isn't working or that the worst-case scenario will occur. Remember, it doesn't have to be true. Believing it's true is all that matters in your world.

Not only can self-curse-talk ruin a promising day, it can also destroy an entire life of promise. Many gifted and talented people don't achieve their goals or fulfill their potential because they keep hearing and replaying the same recording in their heads over and over again:

"This just isn't going to work."

"I just don't have the money and never will."

"I'm not lucky."

"I better play it safe."

"I can't believe how stupid I am."

"This happens every time I try to improve my life!"

The spell has been cast, and the culprit is you. People who have a proclivity for self-curse-talk use it in virtually everything they do, empowering an already negative belief system and solidifying toxic labels influencing the unfolding of the story of their lives.

The bottom line is this: the power of your beliefs is immense. It can motivate you, lift you up and take you to the highest highs, or it can drag you down to the lowest lows.

Shift Your Thoughts & Magically Change Your World

How do we break away from the tired treadmill of our "woe is me" stories? How do we keep ourselves from feeling victimized every time some situation in our lives doesn't turn out the way we want it to? First of all, as I've emphasized, you have to become aware of what you are doing to yourself. You can't remedy a negative situation if you're not aware of what you are doing to yourself and its consequences. You have to be Aware of the Awareness. You have to understand that your thoughts and emotions are caught up in a vicious cycle that is causing you to veer out of control.

Once you recognize this is your M.O. and that you are not feeling right, you are now in a state of awareness. A state of awareness is a good place to be, because all negative chatter ceases. This is your window of opportunity to methodically shift your way of thinking and choose thoughts that will gradually make you feel better, in the moment and for the long term. This is not a "snap-yourself-back-into-a-good-mood" process. It's not about going instantly from an emotionally distraught state to a joyful one. That's just not possible— your brain would probably pop.

The key word to remember is "gradual." It is a thought-by-thought process that gradually makes you feel better and better until, finally, you've calmed your nervous system down and can view the situation at hand from a higher perspective. When you are caught up in a whirlwind of negative drama, not only are negative thoughts building and feeding off each other, but the longer you focus on what was not working, the more power you give them. You could say that you're on a negative rampage, and this rampage is causing you to feel totally helpless and out of control.

Let's go back to the example where Charlie was on a negative rampage, okay? Oh, don't give me a hard time. Just say "okay"! Okay? Well, okay then.

If, at some point during Charlie's meltdown, he were to become aware of what he was doing to compound a challenging situation, if he were to acknowledge that his negativity was feeding upon itself, and if he were to come to understand the consequences of remaining in that emotional state, he could then choose to methodically shift his way of thinking and create thoughts that would make him feel better and get motivated to move forward.

"Wow, I have to calm down. I'm making this worse than what it really is. Why do I do this to myself? I have a meeting with a client today. It's important that I'm in the right frame of mind. I know from past experience that being irate and upset won't get me what I want. In fact, it will only make the situation worse. I have a responsibility not only to myself, but to the client and the company. They're probably giving me all of this stuff to do because they think I'm capable. Plus, they only want me to speak for fifteen minutes or so. Yes, I'll probably be nervous, but I think I can handle it. I guess I should feel honored that they asked me. You know what? I am more than capable."

Does that sound like the most unrealistic inner dialogue ever? Maybe. But just one of those thoughts could be enough to get Charlie motivated to take control of the situation. This shift in thinking will actually bring solutions to his current situation. The more you attempt to create positive thoughts, the more positive your reality will become. Even the slightest shift in thinking will give you a feeling of relief and start you on your way to finding a solution.

So, let's briefly recap this section about your feelings. If you find yourself in a situation that is triggering a negative rampage, STOP, take a breath and remind yourself that your habitual negative thought patterns are causing you to feel bad and distorting the reality of what is happening. When you realize that you have a choice as to how you view any given situation, you can then take actions to feel better.

Remember, the moment you become Aware that you are entering into The Negative Zone, the negativity stops. At that moment, think of the repercussions should you allow this negative rampage to continue. Know that this is your window of opportunity, for within that State of Awareness lies a world of possibility that can launch the wheels of motivation full speed ahead.

Once you start to feel better, a brighter outcome will prevail. When you acknowledge your experience and the change that occurred because of the different actions you took, you have taken one more step in the process of building the successful and happy life you want. ■

Common Sense Success Strategy

SHIFT Your Way of Thinking

Once you become aware that you're not feeling right and recognize that your thoughts are causing your emotions to snowball out of control, methodically choose thoughts that will make you feel better.

If you can master this habit, you can master your life.

4

Enjoyment: A Shift into High Gear

IF *FEELING GOOD* IS THE FUEL THAT DRIVES MOTIVATION, then *enjoyment* shifts motivation into high gear. In my view, if you are not enjoying yourself during the process of achieving your goals, it will be nearly impossible to stay motivated in the long haul.

Unfortunately, in this day and age, enjoyment seems to be something that many of us leave by the wayside—especially when change is taking place at a tremendous rate and the pressure is on to reinvent ourselves and achieve new goals. Or when there are tight deadlines to be met and things aren't going as planned. Now, more than ever, we are having difficulty balancing our lives, and there just doesn't seem to be enough time to get everything done. That's when the stress level can get too intense and negative emotions such as self-doubt, anger, fear and being overwhelmed can become dangerous mindsets. Without realizing it, we allow enjoyment and our ability to laugh and have fun to become secondary at a time when they're most necessary.

Studies have shown that those who make conscious choices to enjoy themselves and laugh throughout the day (and it is a choice) are more creative, productive and resilient. They are also more likely to easily find solutions to complex problems. In other words, focusing on your happiness not only makes you smarter, it shifts motivation into high gear. How smart and how motivated are you?

We allow enjoyment and our ability to laugh and have fun to become secondary at a time when they're most necessary.

It just makes sense that if you are enjoying the process—if you choose to be happy—the odds will be in your favor that you'll stay motivated and achieve your desired outcomes. But I would wager any amount of money that, when writing out their short- or long-term goals, most people don't count enjoying themselves during the process as part of the equation. Instead, they fall prey to dangerous mindsets. They put their happiness on hold when they repeat and internalize negative statements like, "I'll enjoy myself when I get the job done," "I'll be happy when I'm appreciated," or "I'll be happy when I make more money." And, of course, the Big Kahuna: "I'll enjoy myself when I reach a certain status in life." Wow! The pressure we put on ourselves…

For some people (especially high achievers), it seems a virtue to defer happiness and enjoyment. I'm reminded of the phrase "All good things come to those who wait." Let's discuss this nugget of wisdom, shall we? This phrase implies that the end result is the only place where happiness resides. I disagree. Granted, patience is a virtue. I understand that more often than not we have to wait to reap the fruits of our labor. But at the expense of being happy? Really?

Back in my stand-up comedy days, I knew many comics who put their happiness on hold. They had difficulty enjoying the process because they believed they wouldn't be happy until they signed with HBO, got their own sitcom…or their own movie deal…or whatever. I know, because I was one of them.

Over the years, I've seen close friends—comedians—morph into bitter, jealous and resentful people who no longer enjoyed making people laugh. Without ever realizing what they were doing to themselves, they got caught up in their own quest to become a star, which, in their minds was the only thing that would make them happy. The world of show business became their only business. Their total existence revolved around getting discovered, which was ironic because they had no idea how lost they really were.

It was disheartening to see that they never allowed themselves the time to fully appreciate the process or to find value in other aspects of themselves. Theirs was a shallow existence. They would perform from club to club and go from one audition to the next. Their lives were on automatic pilot as they strived with little enthusiasm and waited for that big break, that day somewhere in the future when they would finally be fulfilled. Nothing stifles motivation more than just merely going through the motions and waiting for your life to happen.

I understand how easy it is for us to get so caught up in the hustle and bustle of trying to make a living that we forget what it's like to live. I know that sometimes life consumes us to the point where we allow ourselves to become imprisoned by personal dramas and become blind to all the good that is in our lives. But who says we can't at least try to acquire a healthier attitude and look for the joy in and around our challenges and setbacks.

Trust me when I say there are always more bills to pay and something expensive to repair around the house. Unexpected setbacks will occur and new work projects and goals will quickly replace the ones that are currently stressing you out. Statements that focus on what you lack in the present or predicate on happiness on a future event not only destroy your chance of enjoying the moment, but literally stifle you.

Think about it…It's impossible to get yourself motivated if you're constantly focusing on what isn't working in your life. It's impossible to go through the day with an unstoppable attitude to succeed if you're always complaining about what you don't have. And it's impossible to enjoy the process if you are waiting for some future event before you can be happy! Got it?

Let's say you are having a tough time enjoying the day and getting motivated. Your mind is reeling with all sorts of complaints and negative self-talk.

"Right now, there are just too many things happening in my life."

"I've got too many changes taking place."

"My job is absolutely driving me out of my mind."

"I just learned how to work that stupid software and now they're telling me that I have to learn a whole different system. Why can't they make up their minds? I'll tell you why! Because nobody cares about my needs, that's why! I am not appreciated and I certainly don't get the respect I deserve!"

"When things calm down and my life starts working the way I want, I'll allow myself to enjoy things."

I think it's fair to say you need an attitude adjustment. Take positive steps to reverse that human instinct to withhold happiness from yourself or else your ability to feel good and enjoy life will always be at least one step ahead of you.

The good news is there are always fresh opportunities to feel good and be happy. Imagine life is like Grand Central Station, where such opportunities arrive around the clock. Chances are, one has already arrived. It could be right in front of you. Shift your focus so you can notice and appreciate it. When you do so, your perspective changes. There is absolutely no reason why you can't plan for the future, set goals, undergo your daily routine, deal with the unexpected and still make conscious choices to feel good and enjoy yourself while doing so. If you do, you will not only be producing the fuel that drives motivation, you will be shifting motivation into high gear.

Your Overall Happiness

Now before we go any further, let me make this perfectly clear. I'm in no way suggesting that if you make feeling good a habit and use the strategies I'm offering that you will live happily ever after 24/7, 365 days a year. Give me a break. This is not a prescription for antidepressants or a Disney movie. To expect to be happy and to feel good all the time is to set yourself up for disappointment and failure. Furthermore, if you were happy and feeling good all of the time, the meaning would be completely lost because you would have nothing to compare it with.

Let's face it. Even the very fortunate among us will always have challenges and unexpected problems to deal with, and sometimes we're just going to be in a bad mood. Challenges and stress are a part of life. My point is you can still be happy overall—if you choose to be. Every day. That's the key.

A few years ago, I spent four wonderful days at the Four Seasons Hotel in Kona, Hawaii, where I had the pleasure of being the keynote speaker for a wonderful group of Top Sales Performers and spouses of a well-known financial group. My job was to give them the tools they needed to embrace change and the intense growth they were undergoing and would inevitably continue to see in the coming years. Quality customer service was a priority. I knew the tension was high, but I was prepared.

One morning, two hours before my speech, I was having breakfast at a restaurant with a captivating view of the ocean. As the waitress was pouring my coffee, I asked, "Why is it that no matter where they are, or what they are doing, Hawaiian people always seem to be happy and at peace with themselves? Is there some kind of secret that I should know about?"

She laughed and looked around as if to make sure no one was listening and, in a low voice, replied, "Mr. Rizzo, today is your lucky day. For today I will tell you the secret that most Hawaiian people live by." She sat down in the chair next to mine, motioned for me to get closer and handed me a laminated card from her pocket on which was printed some text. "This is for you," she said. "It really is a secret that should be shared with everyone."

The card read, *"Don't wait for the storms of your life to pass. Learn to dance in the rain."*

Read that again, my friend. That statement is a touchstone for living a successful, happier life, especially when you are experiencing intense change and growth of any kind. That, in part, is the message I shared with the financial group.

When the storms of life are pouring down on you, muster up the courage to **dance** and bless the things that life has given you. The alternative is to **drown** as you curse your challenges and unfortunate circumstances. I don't know about you, but I'll take **dancing** over **drowning** any day!

Understand that experiencing true happiness invariably involves emotional discomfort and difficult experiences along the way. In fact, it relies on them. Challenges build character and self-esteem. How we approach and respond to challenges is what determines how we feel and the quality of our happiness. Happy and successful people can experience highs and lows throughout their lives while maintaining a positive outlook. The goal isn't to be in a perpetual state of Pollyannaish happiness. Rather, the goal is to realize that if you can stay conscious of your ability to shift into a feel good state of mind, you will stay motivated. I will show you how to do this a little later on in the book.

For now, I want you to understand that you can teach yourself to appreciate the benefits of temporarily stepping away from your feelings of being overwhelmed and shift your attention to that which empowers you. Why wait for a problem to be solved or a challenge to go away before you can allow yourself to feel good? Why not learn to exercise positive alternatives that will enable you to feel confident? Why wait for some future goal to be fulfilled in order to be happy? *Why aren't you answering me?* Seriously, read this paragraph again. It's a major key to staying motivated throughout the day.

If you really think about it, it defies all logic. I mean, what good is achieving a goal or even setting a goal for yourself if you don't enjoy the process of fulfilling it? When you make feeling good and being happy of paramount importance, you will feel good no matter what your circumstances or the outcome of the problems you are facing. Remember, the better you feel, the happier you are. The happier you are, the more motivated you become. The more motivated you become, the easier it is to get what you want—and that is to achieve your goals. ■

5

The Greatest Motivator of All

AS YOU HAVE SEEN THROUGHOUT THIS BOOK, your ability to view a stressful or painful situation from a healthier perspective is the ultimate empowerment. Whether you know it or not, the reason you gain this empowerment is because you have made a connection, either consciously or subconsciously, to the greatest motivator of all…Your Higher Self.

This chapter is about acknowledging that there is more to our existence than our human and physical selves. There is a higher part of us, a force, a powerful energy involved in our lives, and if we adhere to this higher part, then life becomes easier to embrace, both at home and at work.

It really doesn't matter what you call this part of yourself. You can call it your Higher Self, God, the Light, the Force (especially if you're Jedi), Love, Source, the Power, the Almighty, Bob. Or Anita. Whatever. The name you give it does not diminish its power in your life.

When I'm connected to this higher part of myself, my attitude and motivational skills are at peak performance. I'm calm on the inside and confident to forge ahead, regardless of the chaos and injustices that may be taking place all around me. When I'm not connected, my attitude is off and I lack the motivation to get things done. Even the slightest disturbance can seem like an insurmountable task. It's about as simple as that.

Sometimes I'm so caught up in life, so busy paying bills, catching planes, making decisions, writing books about being busy, achieving goals and trying to balance my life that I don't live in compliance with the higher part of myself. When I don't, there is usually hell to pay. We all create our own hell when, for whatever reason, we don't make the shift to view our challenges from a higher part of ourselves. Every time we think, feel or choose to act in a negative way, we run the risk of separating ourselves from our natural state of joy and inner peace. The price we pay for this is the burning inner conflict that leads to physical duress and a host of mental and emotional disorders. If every destructive thought you have kills a part of you in some way (AND IT DOES!), you can imagine what it does to motivation.

When you allow yourself to go on emotional binges of anger, guilt, hatred, jealousy and fear, you are punishing yourself by inducing pain, sickness and failure. Yes, you might feel you have every right to complain and to rant and rave about how unfair your life is. It may even seem justified not to forgive someone who deliberately you put in harm's way. Just remember that you also have a right to the migraine headaches, stomach disorders, high blood pressure and miserable existence that inevitably follow.

6

Motivation + Life Balance = Happiness

"Make conscious choices to periodically step away from your job and shift your attention to neglected parts of yourself that are yearning to be expressed."
— STEVE RIZZO *(That's me)*

SOMETIMES WE GET SO CAUGHT UP IN THE DAILY DRAMA of our jobs and become so determined to get what we think we want that we bypass what we need to be truly successful and happy. This type of mindset runs the risk of focusing our attention and motivation primarily on our professional goals, leaving other crucial parts of ourselves by the wayside. More often than not, on our road to success, we neglect the subtle messages or warning signs that a higher part of ourselves is trying to convey to us. These messages could very well be the missing ingredients that complete you as a person. It's really just a matter of becoming aware and listening to what your soul is trying to tell you. Remember, what you *want* in life usually feeds the ego. What you *need* feeds the soul. It would be wise to occasionally ask yourself, "Which one am I feeding now?"

Years ago I was watching a Barbara Walters special on television. She was interviewing a major personal comedic influence of mine, Johnny Carson. Of course, Johnny Carson was an inspiration to an entire generation of performers. As the host of *The Tonight Show*, Carson spent thirty years as the top dog in television comedy. To me, at least, it seemed like no one on Earth could have been happier and more successful, and I tuned in eagerly to hear what such a fortunate man might say.

The interview came during Carson's last year as the host. As you may know, Barbara Walters has a reputation of being very direct when interviewing celebrities, but if anyone could handle The Woman Who Pulls No Punches, I thought surely it would be The King of Late Night Television.

In the end, I was surprised, shocked even, at the way Johnny responded to Walters' questions. I expected the carefree attitude of a man who had conquered the world and was going out on top. Instead of the usual barrage of rapid-fire jokes and wisecracks when he was questioned about his personal life, he gave short, awkward replies that didn't at all suggest confidence. There was an aura of melancholy about him that I believe even took Barbara Walters by surprise.

At the end of the interview, Walters alluded to Carson's fame and long list of accomplishments, any of which were far greater than I, as an up and coming comedian, could have imagined attaining. Then she asked one last question: "Are you happy?"

I couldn't help myself. I blurted out, "What a stupid question! Of course, he's happy, he's Johnny Carson!" I was shocked, though, when Carson stumbled uncomfortably.

"I don't know," he said. "I honestly don't know."

Why, I wondered, was someone who gave so much joy and laughter to millions of people four and five days a week for almost thirty years unable to answer the question, "Are you happy?" Maybe he was in a low mood because he was leaving a TV show that was a great part of his life. I could buy that. Anyone would be sad under similar circumstances. But even after being reminded of his accomplishments in the television and entertainment industry and the monumental impact he made in people's lives, he still couldn't answer the question. On the final episode of *The Tonight Show*, Johnny gave his farewell address to the millions who were watching. It was then that the reason why was evident. Let me explain.

Most people would say that Johnny Carson had the world in the palms of his hands back then. Perhaps that shouldn't be anyone's focus. What really matters is not only the realization that you always hold your own world in your hands, but that you are also responsible for the choices you make as you're holding it. Your entire life is based on the choices you make. Some are made consciously, while others are made unconsciously. Either way, there are always consequences. This is not a threat, but a universal fact. We would all stand a better chance to live a happier life if we were more conscious of, and put some thought behind, our choices. The problem is that many of our choices are made unconsciously; therefore, we don't perceive them as choices. Believe me, they are. In fact, everything that is occurring in your life at this moment is a result of choices you made in the past. Those choices—conscious or unconscious—are key factors that determine your quality of life right now. I have you thinking now, don't I?

On that final episode of *The Tonight Show*, Carson said, "I am one of the lucky ones in the world. I found something I always wanted to do and enjoyed every minute of it."

I'm sure he did. But not too long after that statement he revealed deep regret and apologized to his sons Kit and Cory for "not being there enough," adding that he loved them. He also expressed sorrow and guilt about the death of his son Richard, who died in a car crash in 1991.

Let us not forget that Johnny was married four times. His ex-wives were often the butt of his jokes. Behind the mask of humor, was there someone who truly wanted a lasting relationship? It was apparent that he was so caught up in his role as The King of Late Night Television that he had difficulty identifying himself with anything or anyone else.

It's obvious that Johnny Carson gave much and received much, but paid heavily. It makes one wonder, is there always a price to pay when what we do for a living becomes our whole life, no matter what level of success we achieve? We have to ask ourselves, is the price worth it? And, is there a way to find a happy balance and disburse our attention and motivation to other aspects of our lives that are waiting to be nourished.

Are You Married to Your Job?

Not too long ago, I was sitting on a beach in San Juan, Puerto Rico, and noticed a couple holding hands, walking along the shoreline. They looked so peaceful, like an advertisement for an island getaway. Then it happened: his cell phone went off. She gave him a look as if to say, "I dare you!" I couldn't believe it. The idiot took the dare. Not only did he answer the phone, but he let go of her hand, walked away and talked for about ten minutes. She shook her head, walked over to their beach setup, which was about twenty feet from mine, and sat down under their umbrella. By now, the couple that looked like an advertisement for an island getaway was about to become a prime candidate for the Dr. Phil show.

He walked over to her and tried to explain. I grimaced. In my head, I heard the booming catchphrase popularized by announcer Michael Buffer that boxing fans know so well:

"Let's get ready to ruuuumble!"

Ding, ding! She came out swinging.

"How could you?" she asked. "I can't even believe you brought your cell phone with you, but you had the nerve to answer it!"

What he should have done now was listen to what she had to say. Of course, he didn't.

"Hey!" he jabbed at her in his defense. "If it wasn't for my business, we wouldn't even be on this vacation!"

She rebounded with a combination of blows that seemed to shake the champ. "Vacation?" she said, incredulous. "You call this a vacation? This is our anniversary! We've been here for three days so far and you can't stay away from your cell phone and stupid computer! You brought your job with you! It's like you're addicted!"

She picked up her belongings and took a few steps toward the hotel. Then she stopped, turned and delivered the haymaker:

"You know, you used to be married to me. Now you're married to your job!" The champ just stood there looking like a real chump. I thought the wife made an interesting choice of words.

Does this story come as a surprise? Let's face it. We are living in a world that is moving at an amazing pace. It is easy to get lost and misplace our feelings and values. Most of us are conditioned to devote most of our waking hours and motivational skills to our jobs and professional goals leaving little, if any, time for other important aspects of our lives. Who can deny that we live in a highly competitive society that stresses the importance of being the very best rather than simply doing the best we can? Many have bought into the grand deception of always wanting more, regardless of what they already have.

If you are not enjoying yourself on your journey toward your goals, you're ripping yourself off.

We have adopted the illusion that money, power and fame can fill that self-created emptiness and make us feel complete. I am not suggesting that there is anything wrong with these things, but our obsession with them makes them dangerous, especially when we allow ourselves to neglect other aspects of our lives.

Perhaps we should redefine success. If you consult a dictionary, you will see what I mean. I find it absolutely amazing that the words "happiness" and "joy" are not included in the definition of "success." Unfortunately, our conventional definition is simply achieving the goal. Little thought is devoted to the value of experiencing the journey, building character and learning life lessons along the way— all of which are crucial elements in nourishing the soul. Very few people ever consider the grave consequences of remaining joyless throughout the process.

You see, it really doesn't matter how much money you have, how famous you are or how many goals you've achieved. It makes no difference how big your house is or what industry accolades you've racked up in your career. The entire world can view your life as the ultimate success story, but the bottom line is this: **If you are not happy, you are not successful!** If you are not enjoying yourself on your journey toward your goals, you're ripping yourself off. Trust me. There are enough people willing to do that for you.

What am I getting at? I'll tell you. As I alluded to earlier, maybe it would be wise for us to come to the realization that what we think we want in life may not necessarily be what we need in order to lead a truly successful and happy life. Maybe, just maybe, we are leaving out important factors from the equation of what truly completes us as individuals. Maybe it's just a matter of making a slight shift, finding your balance and choosing a better way. Maybe there are too many "maybes" in this paragraph.

Yes, indeed, our lives depend on the choices we make, but I believe we can at least minimize our regrets just by being more consciously aware of our choices. This is what the habit of shifting your focus in order to be happy moment to moment does for you. Before you know it, you actually *are* happy. Then it becomes clear what you should focus on in the big picture.

I love the Spanish proverb, "God says, 'Choose what you will and pay for it.'" It stresses that life holds no easy answers, only choices. Sometimes they are costly. We must live with and pay for the consequences. I don't know what type of business the guy on the beach was in that consumed so much of his time, but it was apparent that the scene between him and his wife was not an isolated incident. I would wager any amount of money that they have had this discussion many times before. After all, he was clearly unable to shift his focus. He *was* married to his job.

Here is a question I want you to ponder in that brain of yours. I really want you to seriously consider what I am suggesting here before you answer. Are you ready? Is it possible that you are focusing so much of your time and energy on the success of your job or career that you are unconsciously leaving out important elements that would otherwise bring you joy and make your life complete? Keep reading, my friend. ■

7

Shift Your Motivation & Honor Your Values

ONE OF MY RESPONSIBILITIES AS A MOTIVATOR is to show people how to acquire the attitude they need to be happy and successful on all levels of life while enjoying the process. When I write "happy and successful on all levels of life," I mean just that. Your personal and professional lives make up the whole of you. If you put most of your time and energy on one area, you run the risk of leaving the other unfulfilled. This is especially common among high achievers—perhaps you, dear reader.

Someone once said, "Hectic minds create a hectic world." Every now and then we just have to stop the hectic world and get off for a while. We must never be too busy to take time out from our job and experience sacred parts of ourselves that are so often buried and yearning to be expressed. When our jobs consume us, eventually, in one form or another, there will be a price to pay. I'm not suggesting that we shouldn't love what we are doing for a living. In fact, it's important that we do. And it is essential that we devote quality time toward our job. The problem arises when what we do for a living interferes with our other precious core values. A value can be tangible or intangible, like health and fitness, honesty, truthfulness, freedom, courage, spirituality, beauty, goodness, playfulness, self-sufficiency, wealth, time to spend as we like, and so on. These cherished values need to be experienced and expressed. They give us self-worth. Ignoring them for too long can only lead to unhappiness, regardless of how prestigious your profession is, how much money you make or how successful you think you are.

Below are some examples of cherished values that are often neglected or buried because of our jobs:

+ **Spending more time with my family.** I really enjoy spending time at home. I love quality time with my children—playing with them, helping them with their homework and getting to know them. I love my job, but it hurts that I am missing out on valuable time with my loved ones time that I know I will never get back. I am going to have to cut down on volunteering for assignments and working late. I want to occasionally leave early so I can have more time for them. When I get home too late, I know that I missed out on something very special, and I don't like going to bed feeling guilty.

+ **Taking a weekend off from work, without interruption and free from emails, cell phones and text messages.** I'm sick of taking my job home with me! I just want to be alone, hang out in my sweats and not care how I look. I want to be able to do what I want, read a book, watch a great movie (even a crappy one!), listen to music, work in my garden or just sleep. I miss this part of myself, and I'm taking it back.

✦ **Doing the things that connect me to my spirit.** Yes, things are going great at work. I've been recognized as "salesman of the year" three years in a row. I'm producing more than I ever could have imagined. I am truly blessed for the financial wealth I have accumulated over the years. But my spiritual reservoir is on empty. Taking time to commune with nature is important to me. I can't remember the last time I went hiking or even walked through a scenic area. I barely have time to meditate or to appreciate a sunrise or sunset the way I used to. I guess I just got caught up. Yes, I'm successful, but I don't feel fulfilled. I have to bring that sacred part of myself back. There's no reason I can't do that and still continue my success at work. I deserve to be happy on all levels.

When we finally become aware that our jobs are interfering with sacred parts of ourselves, we can then choose to find ways to shift our attention and motivate ourselves to bring our values into existence. The result: we raise our self-worth, increase self-respect and reduce the gap between aspiring for fulfillment and actually feeling fulfilled, thus reducing the risk of burnout. Now, that's not only what I call nourishing your soul—it's the ultimate success!

I understand that it's far too easy to ignore these valued parts of yourself when you're caught up in your job and struggling to succeed. Nevertheless, they could very well be the main ingredients that make up the recipe of your life. One of those ingredients could be the missing link that soothes your hectic mind and fulfills your world with the happiness you desire. The amazing thing is that most of the time it's just a simple matter of becoming aware of what is missing and then making the appropriate choices to fix it. "She'll understand," you may tell yourself. "She knows how much I love her. We'll spend more time together when things settle down at work. After all, I'm doing this for both of us." I promise you that's what the chump on the beach was telling himself.

Are you nurturing your artistic talents or hobbies, such as painting, photography, crafts, gardening, music, etc., or have you lost your way on the road to success?

When your little boy or girl is saying, "Hey, look at me!" are you really paying attention, or is your mind on what needs to be done tomorrow at the office? You will never have that moment again. Remember, sometimes it's not what you do that causes you regret. It could very well be what you don't do that comes back to haunt you.

Your soul is continually yearning to be fulfilled and nourished. It takes more than just driving to succeed in your profession and overcoming obstacles to feed it. We must also take time out from the hustle and bustle of our everyday lives and feel the joy and simplicity that life has to offer.

Your soul is continually yearning to be fulfilled and nourished.

Sometimes I think that if my soul had a voice it would say, "Excuse me, Steve? I understand that part of soul work is honoring your pain and grief. I know you have responsibilities. I know you have goals and dreams. I know you have bills to pay. I also know that life has thrown many challenges your way and that, for the most part, you handle them quite well. In fact, it makes me feel wonderful that you're learning life's lessons. But can you please stop for a while and connect with what really gives you joy? Might I suggest that you go to the child within you that used to be so close to me and rediscover what truly makes you happy and gives you peace of mind? And can you please care enough about yourself to find a place for those things in your life? In other words, my friend Steve, what about *my* needs? After all, my needs and yours are one and the same."

Forget for a moment the fact that my soul sounds like James Earl Jones. I'm more than aware that there are many people who find great value and fulfillment in their occupations. My profession—helping people to shift their mindsets in order to find success and happiness—absolutely fulfills a sacred part of me. However, my job does not make up my whole life.

Understand that I'm not asking you to ignore your professional goals, joys and responsibilities. They, too, are sacred parts of you that foster soul growth. I know all too well that our professional goals and responsibilities quite often require sacrifice, dedication and countless hours of overtime. I'm simply asking you *not* to ignore other sacred parts of yourself that complete you. It's called balancing your life, and achieving it is often just a matter of adjustment and motivation.

Shift Your Priorities

Write a list of things that you truly value and bring you joy, such as quality time with family and friends, solitude, playfulness, spirituality, walking, nature, health, a hobby, traveling, artistic ability and so on. Spend at least half an hour, and really dig deep. If you're thorough and honest with yourself, you may be surprised to discover that your current way of living doesn't allow much room for these things. If this is so, my friend, it's time to make different choices and tweak your life accordingly. Whatever you do, don't make this too difficult and don't berate yourself for screwing up. You didn't screw up. (Unless you answered your cell phone on the beach, moron.) For the most part, you were just caught up in the thing we call life. We all make unconscious choices and respond to situations without even thinking of the long-term consequences.

Now you have a wonderful opportunity to take some time and contemplate how you can shift your priorities around to fulfill your needs. This may take a few mental adjustments, like picturing where your couch will go in a new apartment. Imagine what effort it would take to find fulfillment in each value on the list. Imagine the benefits of taking a few extra hours out of the week to devote to any of the activities and how good that might make you feel. Listen to your heart, use common sense and steer yourself toward the things that lift you up and bring you joy. What I'm telling you here is teach yourself to become consciously aware of what you truly value, then make the appropriate choices and motivation to fulfill those needs.

This is where "free will" comes back into play. Whenever you are in a situation where you are trying to bring professional and personal balance into your life, ask yourself the three free-will "will" questions:

1. *Will* there be personal consequences to this choice I'm making?

2. *Will* this choice affect others, now and in the future?

3. *Will* this choice make me happy, now and in the future?

The answer to the first two questions will always be "yes," whether you know it or not. The third question, I don't have to tell you, is the most important. By asking yourself the first two questions, you've answered "yes" and thought about the ramifications of your decision. The third question is all about you, though. Will it make you happy? It's simple. Answer it. Your answer may end up guiding you to a decision, especially after forcing yourself to consider the consequences that will arise from answering differently.

These three questions don't guarantee that you will always make the best choice; however, they are very empowering in that they allow you to stand behind the helm of your life and see more clearly how to steer the course of events, situations and circumstances you encounter.

There are those who insist that they can't afford to spend time outside of the realm of their careers. In actuality, when you think of the consequences, you really can't afford not to. Taking time off is not a waste of time. It's time well spent. When you step away from the worry and chaos that so often comes with success, you are not only nourishing other parts of yourself, you are energizing your spirit and recharging your motivational battery to go back to work.

My friend Victoria was so caught up in climbing the corporate ladder, deadlines, overtime and working weekends that she was neglecting something of great value that always brought her great joy and lifted her spirits: her friends. She couldn't remember the last time she spent quality time with them. It really was a simple matter of picking up the phone, inviting them to dinner or spending the weekend together. Now they all make it a special occasion once a month or so. By the way, Victoria is still climbing the corporate ladder—only now she does it without neglecting a sacred part of herself. She made the shift and is now nourishing her soul by sharing experiences with like-minded people. In her words, "I feel refreshed and complete whenever we spend time together."

My Time

I put a great deal of time and energy into building my career. There always seems to be something that needs to be done—new projects to be worked on in the way of books, products and customizing programs for clients. The more engagements I complete, the more in-demand I become as a speaker. Now don't misunderstand me. This is not a complaint. I really do love and enjoy what I do. It feels good to provide services that are in need, and I feel that I do them well. The important thing is what I choose to do when I'm not in front of an audience or working on new programs. After a lifetime of worry, frustration and disappointment in little shortcomings, I am now beginning to understand how valuable that time in between is. I call it: "MY TIME." And with MY TIME, I simply do what makes me happy. I have found that the amount of MY TIME isn't as important as the attention I give it. In other words, it's quality time that matters, not quantity. This time can be a day or a few weeks at home in between bookings, or it can be the simple luxury of staying overnight at a hotel before I give a morning speech. Whatever the amount of time I have, it's what I choose to do with it that brings it value. I try to make conscious choices to feed my soul and complement parts of myself that need fostering and make me happy.

Your job is not who you are, it's what you do. What you do for a living may be a sacred part of who you are, but, on its own merits, it doesn't complete you.

For example, whether I'm home or on the road, I always find time to exercise. Always! It simply makes me feel great physically, emotionally, mentally and spiritually. Sometimes when I'm away from home I may choose to go for a walk through a historical neighborhood. I discovered years ago that walking is a form of meditation that always puts my mind at ease. Quite often, as I'm walking, solutions to problems hit me with such clarity that I have to laugh. (You might want to try that the next time you're all stressed out over a problem at work.) Perhaps I may choose to stay in my hotel room and take a nap or read a book. I've become accustomed to both. Something else I love to do when I'm traveling is to meet with friends for dinner and indulge in great conversation, nonstop laughter and, of course, a great bottle of wine or two or three. Don't give me that look! There's always a designated driver.

These are just some of the things that complete me as a person. To you, they may seem simple or unproductive, even boring. But, to me, they are essential to my well-being. MY TIME is when I let go of the hectic world and find my balance. Here is where I achieve a profound understanding that I don't have to push life so much in order to experience it harmoniously, to be guided more by intuition than ambition. Some of my greatest insights have come to me when I have decided to simply break away and pay attention to who I am.

Your job is not who you are, it's what you do. What you do for a living may be a sacred part of who you are, but, on its own merits, it doesn't complete you. There's so much more to you than what you do to earn a paycheck. Deep inside, you know this is true.

By all means, dedicate a great amount of time toward achieving your professional goals. But for your sake, learn how to let go and honor those other sacred parts of yourself. If you do, don't be surprised if you find that you are more passionate, enthusiastic and motivated at work. Allow yourself the freedom to use your time to love, laugh and learn. Find your balance! Find your joy! Live your life with passion! Don't be afraid to shift your life in the direction of the things that you value and that nourish your soul. Shift your focus when you are feeling fragmented and upset to bring yourself back to your higher sense of being, and shift your priorities to allow yourself to focus on what matters.

When shift happens, your life changes. And trust me, my friend. It's for the better. ■

Common Sense Success Strategy

Make conscious choices to periodically step away from your job and experience other parts of yourself that are yearning to be expressed. Notice how much better you feel about this new balance you have created.

Remember, I'm not asking you to ignore your professional responsibilities. I'm simply asking you not to ignore other sacred parts of yourself that just might fulfill and complete you.

8

Start Each Day with an Unstoppable Attitude!

RIGHT NOW YOU MIGHT BE THINKING, *"Great, Steve. All of this stuff about feeling good and enjoying yourself makes sense, but how can you feel good and enjoy yourself when nothing in your life seems to be working? I mean, there are a lot of people out there that have a great deal of stuff to deal with. Some are experiencing financial problems. Some are going through a bitter divorce. What if there's an illness in the family? What if your life just isn't going the way you want? How in the world can you expect anyone to feel good, let alone enjoy life, when they have so much crap and stress to deal with every day?!"*

These are all valid questions. Here is the answer. Drugs! Just kidding! These types of questions are often brought up when I give my workshops and seminars.

What you are about to read from this point on are seven step-by-step Common Sense Success Strategies on how you can start each day with an unstoppable attitude to succeed and how to keep that motivation going throughout the day—every day—regardless of your circumstances.

Remember, this is not Brain Surgery. It's Brain Adjustment. It's about allowing yourself to shift your focus and way of thinking to create lifetime habits that will help you to discover increased productivity, greater enthusiasm and new levels of success in business and in life.

These Common Sense Success Strategies are the foundation on which I built my career and my life. They are responsible for my shift in attitude and keeping me motivated, and they played a crucial role in helping me to overcome the negative labels that I mentioned earlier. I have no doubt that if these transforming strategies can help me they can surely help you.

Right now, I want you to make a conscious choice *every day* to feel good and to enjoy yourself during the process of whatever it is you are trying to achieve. This goes for everything. You can apply this shift in attitude to even the most mundane or unpleasant tasks. Don't reserve it for just your personal and professional goals, but for all your daily chores and choices. Whether you are giving the dog a bath, spending time with your children, cleaning the house, starting an exercise program, watching TV or performing a task at work, make feeling good and enjoying yourself your number one priority. So let's get started! Here's how it works...

the coming day and can't understand why (even after they've had three cups of coffee) their energy level is depleted before they set out to achieve their goals. Think of your responsibilities. Think of the things that need to be done on any given day. Your energy level has to be cranked. Again, that's your choice and your responsibility.

So…What I'm asking you to do is to Get Your SHIFT Together! In other words, when you wake up to greet the day, rather than focusing on what isn't working and all of the things that have to be done, shift your focus to what is working. Shift your way of thinking to the things that lift your spirits, bring you joy and make you feel good. Think of who you have to be in order to handle the challenges of the coming day.

Your only goal as creator is to simply raise your energy level and feel good, whatever that means to you. Focus on the person lying next to you or the comfort of the room, or photographs of happy times with family and friends. Relive one of these wonderful memories or allow your attention to settle on the sound of the birds outside your window or the unfaltering loyalty of the dog lying at the foot of the bed. It can be the achievement of a past goal, your garden, a hobby or the neighborhood you live in. It really doesn't matter what it is, just as long as you hold your attention on it long enough to notice how wonderful it feels to have these things in your life. Dial into your gratitude. Feel it with your heart and soul.

This is important. If you're not really feeling it or if you're forcing it because you need a cup of coffee or you're hungry and want your English muffin, the exercise will be less effective. (Or…You could just be grateful for your cup of coffee and the English muffin you're about to consume!) Consider the act of being truly grateful as if it were a daily vitamin. Commit to something. Gratitude is the most powerful connection you have to your higher self. The stronger the connection, the better you feel. The better you feel, the more creative, productive and motivated you are. When you fully appreciate what you have in the moment, good things come into your life. Why? Because the gratitude bone is connected to the happiness bone, and the happiness bone is connected to the motivation bone. And it's this fun little cycle that eventually acts as a magnet to attract the things you desire most.

Here's my challenge to you: Try this exercise for seven days in a row. Before you get out of bed, focus on how grateful you are for something. Make it part of your waking process and you will engage your subconscious, that great misunderstood mind that basically runs your life. I guarantee that within seven short days you will begin to feel better. It isn't magic; it's taking the steps to create a healthier mindset and making happiness a habit, motivating yourself to create the life you want one day at a time.

This is not Pollyannaish mumbo-jumbo. Scientists and mental health experts teach us that our lives move in the direction of our most dominant thoughts. If you are consistent about creating thoughts about abundance and success and are consciously grateful for the things you already have, you'll not only find yourself moving toward the things you want, you will draw them toward you.

Again, some of you may be thinking that there is too much stress, pain and worry in your life to be grateful for anything. No matter how low you may feel or how bad things are, there is always something to be grateful for. It's your job to dig deep, find it and praise it.

As I said earlier, finding something to be grateful for can take work, but you'll discover it is well worth the effort. Sometimes you have to push yourself, especially when negative emotions about the coming day are getting the best of you. (Does dreading a meeting with the boss ring a bell? If it doesn't, then YOU are probably the boss, so quit giving everybody a hard time!) I have found that when I'm having trouble being grateful, the best thing for me to do is to become absolutely still, dig deep and become aware of the fear, anger, guilt or whatever emotion has its claws in me.

Becoming aware of your negative emotions does not mean that you hold on to them and analyze them with intensity. In fact, it's the complete opposite. It simply means that you observe them without judgment as they pass through your mind. No need to give them any attention. You already know they're bad for you so why attract their attention? This is really a great experience because as you allow the negativity to pass, you actually feel your energy level elevate. Sometimes I have a little fun with this and physically wave to the negative feelings as they leave my body. "Bye-bye," I say, "Have a nice day. I know I will. Don't let the door hit you in the ass on your way out."

Remember, when you become aware of any negative emotion, you actually help break the self-identification you have with it and are able to come back to the present moment. This puts you once again in touch with the power you have to seize the day and realize, once again, that it's all up to you. Hey, that alone is something to be grateful for. Build on that.

Common Sense Success Strategy

Practice shifting into a State of Feeling Good: Whenever you first rise, set your mental stage and emotional gauge to feel good. Know that the creation of your day is about to begin and that you alone are its creator.

Your first decision as creator is to focus on the things that please you and the things you are grateful for. Your goal is to simply raise your energy level to feel good and to give yourself the confidence and attitude you need to stay motivated throughout the day—regardless of your circumstances.

— STRATEGY 3 —

UNLEASH THE POWER OF YOUR HUMOR BEING!

One powerful strategy that can help you to start you day in a good mood is to find the laughter within you and around you. This Strategy should not only start at the beginning of the day, but continue throughout the day, every day.

Did you know that laughter is essential for a healthy and productive workplace? If you didn't, you do now. Whether you are in sales, service, education or any other business, using humor as a strategy in your process will improve morale, increase efficiency and help you create lifelong relationships for success. In other words, laughter is a powerful force to help you stay motivated personally and professionally.

This is why I'm asking you to unleash the power of your Humor Being on a daily basis. Your Humor Being is of your higher self. It's the part that brings out the best in you, especially when times are tough. What your Humor Being can give you more than anything else is emotional stability.

I honestly believe that our ability to shift and occasionally laugh off the major and minor tensions at work and in our lives is crucial in order for us to survive the insanity that surrounds us. I'm not just suggesting this, I'm telling you. We *have* to take time out of each day and laugh. Why do you think people go to comedy clubs, watch sitcoms or see funny movies? Because they want to laugh. Why do they want to laugh? For the same reason that they want to have sex: It simply makes them feel good. A physiological and mental reaction takes place when you laugh. Laughter charges your inner battery and helps you cope with tough times. Even if you are having a really bad day, when you laugh life doesn't seem that bad after all. In fact, a sense of humor can give you strength, courage and the motivation to move forward, even during extreme adversity.

Before describing the characteristics of a Humor Being, let me first define what a sense of humor is. The dictionary says the word *sense* means "perception or awareness; and correct reasoning; or sound judgment." The word *humor* means "turn of mind; to sooth temper or mood; or the mental quality that produces absurd or joyful ideas." So, a sense of humor means to be aware that you have a mental quality to turn your mind in an unusual way, or a need to produce joyful or absurd ideas that can soothe your being. The initiative and proficiency by which you utilize your sense of humor, however, comes from what I call your Humor Being.

Tapping into your Humor Being is a strategy that can help you cope with the natural ups and downs of life. Instead of going through the course of a day allowing unfortunate situations, unlucky circumstances and foul people to suck the energy right out of us, we can turn to our Humor Being for a levity break. Those who make the shift and live in harmony with their Humor Being have the ability to see the bright side of a negative situation, embrace change more easily and make conscious choices to enjoy themselves.

Now, if you're thinking that you can't find the laughter as soon as you wake up to greet the day, you're just not looking. Try looking at yourself first thing in the morning. Really! Don't even get dressed. As soon as you wake up, look into a full-length mirror and say, "Well, I'm ready to go to work just the way I am!" I bet it will at least put a smile on your face.

Humor is everywhere. All you have to do is make the initiative every day to get in sync with your Humor Being and observe. It's what I call observing and developing your humor insights. It simply means observe the funny stuff around you.

If you're married, believe me there is humor there. In fact, I believe that a sense of humor is a major component to having a successful marriage. But, according to *O, The Oprah Magazine*, the key to a successful marriage is to understand you partner. Oh really! Are you kidding me? *Understand* your partner! Whether you are a man or a woman, you will never be able to *understand* your partner! The only thing that you have to *understand* about your partner is that there are things about your partner that you will never *understand*. If you can *understand* that, then you will have better *understanding*. Do you *understand*?

Use your imagination. Observe your kids, especially as you start your day. They are without a doubt the funniest people on earth. Watch how they grow up to be just like you.

My son thinks he's a comedian. When he was in grade school, he was always making people laugh, including the teachers. But he didn't know when to turn it off. This started to become a problem.

One day I came home and said, "How was school today?" Without missing a beat, he said, "Good crowd! Good crowd!"

Trying to hold back my laughter, I said, "Don't get smart with me."

He looked right at me and said, "Don't worry, Pop. I don't want to confuse you."

If you have pets, observe them. They can definitely put a smile on your face. Every cat in the world has a New York attitude. Watch them. They walk around like they're nature's gift to the animal kingdom. I swear, if cats could talk, they would say, "Meow. Meow. Ba-da-bing. Meow!"

It's these types of observations that help you to develop your humor insights. This is how you tap into your laughter reservoirs and how you get your humor genes circulating. This is the stuff that puts you into a good mood. Doesn't it make sense to create this feel good state of mind at the beginning of your day? Hold on to that very special something that made you laugh and take it with you throughout the day. It's so very simple, and the benefits are priceless.

The greatest benefit that comes from observing and developing your humor insights is that you eventually begin to view your challenges and problems from a vantage point rather than from a disadvantage.

Even a little levity can help change how you view a particular problem. I noticed that the more I utilized my Humor Being as a strategy to help me deal with a challenging situation, the more it became a part of who I was and the more emotionally balanced I became. You could say that dealing with life's stressors and problems from a humorous perspective is emotional self-defense—which, in a way, is akin with the principles and conditioning of the martial arts. Let me explain.

Emotional Self Defense

My friend Jeff has a black belt degree in karate. Through years of practice and repetitious training he has conditioned his mind and body to respond automatically against physical attack with a series of self-defense moves consisting of kicks, punches, blocks and throws.

One night at a club a fight broke out. When Jeff tried to break it up, someone attacked him by surprise and punched him in the back of the head. Fortunately for Jeff, the punch didn't make full contact. Without even thinking, he automatically went into his defensive stance, blocked the next punch that was thrown, threw two punches of his own and hurled his assailant through the air and onto the floor.

Here's the cool part. When it was over, Jeff sat down in a chair, brought his hand to his face and said, "Wow! I just got into a fight!" He said he didn't have to think about blocking the next punch or when or how to punch back. It just happened. Now that's conditioning. His mind and body worked together to respond with automatic reflex to keep him from harm's way—to protect his physical self.

In karate, one is constantly practicing their *katas*, which is a series of physical moves such as kicks, punches, jumps and throws. These *katas* condition the student to respond and react effectively in the event of physical attack.

If you make a conscious effort every day to see the humor in the events that attack your emotional well-being, you will be practicing your emotional *kata*. Slowly but surely, you will subconsciously reprogram that brain of yours to the point that when a major emotional attack occurs you will automatically respond to it with more ease. Try it for yourself and see what happens.

Humor is your natural defense mechanism. It's a prescription from your higher self to cure the madness that attacks you from day to day. To deny yourself the right to occasionally to step away from the chaos and find the laughter in the midst of troubling times is like denying yourself treatment that can cure an illness.

Humor & Attitude in the Workplace

Whenever I speak to sales or customer service groups about attitude in the workplace, I always stress the importance of maintaining a healthy state of mind. I make it very clear that there is one thing the people they are doing business with want more than anything else, and that is to *feel good about themselves.* Everything else evolves and revolves around that. The sale, whether they are recommended to others, and all decisions concerning repeat business are based on them *feeling good about themselves.*

Yes, the price and the quality of the product or service you are offering are important. So are your knowledge and expertise, but you won't even make it to first base if they detect that you have negative or uncaring attitude.

In general, this holds true in all relationships. We all want to feel good about ourselves. We are more comfortable and happier in our surroundings when we are with people who have cheerful and optimistic attitudes. It seems to be part of the human condition to want to associate ourselves with those who make us laugh and are fun to be with. It's easier to confide in someone who can make us feel good. We tend to put up walls or try to avoid people who are negative, rude, pushy and always complaining. Why? Because we simply don't feel right.

Here's my point: The people we associate with in the workplace—employees, employers, management, fellow workers or customers—will have a difficult time feeling good about themselves if they sense we have a bad attitude or if they feel that we don't care. And, as I have stated throughout this book, your attitude and the way you feel are always your choice.

Highly successful businesspeople know they are going to have their share of tough times and setbacks. They are well aware that the unexpected can happen at any time. They also know the importance of remaining calm and emotionally stable in the midst of trying times. They intuitively know that a State of Feeling Good is essential in order to stay motivated to find solutions and forge ahead.

You can be an expert in your chosen field. You can have degrees from the finest universities with the highest honors. You can know everything there is to know about your business. None of these things will amount to much unless you have the emotional stability and the motivational skills to deal with unexpected challenges and stressful events, which occur almost every day, in every occupation.

A common scenario is dealing with irrational and rude people who throw their authority around as if the entire world revolved around their needs. If you're not careful, you could leave yourself wide open for emotional attack and allow the other person's attitude to affect your emotional well-being. This, in turn, could cause you to respond to the situation on that person's level, which more than likely would lead to an undesirable result.

Years ago, I was giving a seminar to a large group of Marriott Hotel sales and customer service people on how to start each day with an unstoppable attitude to succeed, regardless of their circumstances. From the corner of my eye I noticed a woman frantically waving—or, should I say, flapping her arms to get my attention. I figured that I'd better ask her what she wanted before she hurt herself or flew out of her seat.

As soon as I acknowledged her, she jumped up and said, "I understand what you're saying, but I'm a manager and sometimes work behind the front desk. I'd like to know how someone is supposed feel good and maintain a healthy state of mind when they are dealing with rude, sarcastic and arrogant people who don't want to hear anything but their own complaints! No matter what you do to try and help, it just doesn't seem to be good enough! You tell me what I'm supposed to do?"

I asked her if this incident recently happened to her. She said that it happened a few days ago and that it still bothered her. Some of the attendees acknowledged the woman's concerns. I listened as others shared their own past experiences in dealing with irate customers. What surprised me were the ones who were still holding onto the anger as if the incident just happened.

I assured them that I understood how a rude or irate customer could cause them to become upset. I also explained that when someone verbally attacks you with demands and insults, it's not just the irate person who is causing you to become distraught, but also your own thoughts about the situation. Furthermore, when you allow a person or a situation to upset you, this is an indication that you are giving up your personal power to choose a better way. You are actually surrendering control of your life and giving that person or situation permission to do what they want with your emotions.

I suggested to everyone that one very effective way to stay in control of a provoking or threatening situation is to turn their Humor Being loose. I then addressed the woman who asked the question and explained that I was going to do a little role-playing. I would play the roles of both the front desk person and the irate customer (whom we will call Mr. Grumpy):

The front desk person is in her office. She hears the pounding of the bell on the front desk. Ding, ding! Ding, ding, ding! Ding, ding, ding, ding!

Front Desk Person: *"Yes sir. Can I help you?"*

Mr. Grumpy: *"I just went to my room and guess what? There's no fireplace! One of the reasons I chose this hotel was because you offered a fireplace! I'm going to be here on business for two weeks! This is not a good way to start off! The reservation was made two months ago! My assistant called a few days ago to confirm the reservation with a fireplace! I'm tired and I want a room with a fireplace and I want it now!"*

Front Desk Person: *"Well sir, I'll check and see what I can do to fix this for you."*

Mr. Grumpy: *"Excuse me! There's nothing to check! You already checked me in! You know I'm supposed to have a room with a fireplace. It's bad enough that I had to wait three hours to check in! Look, I've been in three cities in six days, had two flight cancelations and now this! I'm sick of dealing with people who have no idea what the hell they're doing! I'm going back to my room. (The one without the fireplace.) Call me when my new room (with a fireplace) is ready!"*

After my rant, I took a few bows as I received a big round of applause for my Academy Award-worthy performance. I then addressed the audience and suggested that, in a situation like this, they should excuse themselves and go directly to their office, which is right behind them, take a deep breath and immediately ask their Humor Being for guidance. I then asked them to let loose and mimic the entire situation from a humorous perspective.

When you allow yourself to see the humor in the midst of a stressful or highly emotional situation, your brain is no longer registering negative thoughts that serve to intensify your already out-of-control emotions.

I emphasized that they should use their imagination and go crazy with this, to repeat and exaggerate the same sarcastic words that were spoken. I challenged them to pace back and forth, change the pitch in their voice, animate their movement and go over the entire ordeal as if they were acting in some kind of comedy or cartoon on fast-forward:

Front Desk Person: (mimicking and dancing around the office) "I want a fireplace in my room! I made this reservation two months ago! I waited three hours for this room and when I got there there was no fireplace! Well excuse me, your Majesty! It appears that I made a mistake. I know you've never made a mistake in your entire life! But…unfortunately, I did. (Faster) I'll tell you what I'll do. If for some reason I can't get you a room with a fireplace, I will personally go the nearest hardware store and purchase some bricks and mortar! Then, I will come right back and build you your very own custom-made fireplace, okay?! And if I have one brick left over, do you know what you can do with it? If not, I'll be more than happy to tell you what you can do with it!"

At this point the entire audience was laughing. I explained that this was exactly what they would be doing if they use this methodology. Here's the psychology behind it.

When you allow yourself to see the humor in the midst of a stressful or highly emotional situation, your brain is no longer registering negative thoughts that serve to intensify your already out-of-control emotions. In fact, your brain is now somewhere else, laughing or at least amused at something ridiculous that you just did. So, even when your brain goes back to the situation at hand, you won't feel as overpowered by it as you did before because your laughter has put a stop to the snowball effect. You have calmed down your nervous system to the point where you can actually shift your thoughts to get motivated and pave the way toward a positive outcome. This takes only seconds to do.

Sometimes making the shift to laugh and taking a step back to reassess things with humor seems to be the only remedy to the random craziness of life.

I emphasized to the woman that, after she's calmed down and started feeling more confident, she can leave her office with a healthier attitude and approach Mr. Grumpy with whatever the scenario might be. E.g., "I'm sorry, I don't know what happened. I apologize, but I cannot find you a room with a fireplace this evening. However, tomorrow I can upgrade you to a suite with a fireplace for the remainder of your stay at no additional cost."

I then addressed the entire audience and said that if the customer still isn't satisfied, at least you can say in all honesty that you tried everything in your power to help. Quite often, when we are confronted with someone who is rude and difficult to deal with, it's not always about who's right or who's wrong. It's about advantages and disadvantages. It's about feeling good and at peace in the moment as opposed to anger and chaos. Sometimes making the shift to laugh and taking a step back to reassess things with humor seems to be the only remedy to the random craziness of life.

It truly is amazing the power we derive from stepping outside our emotions and giving ourselves permission to view them from a humorous perspective. You don't have to be a comedian with an arsenal of rapid-fire remarks or wisecracks at your disposal. What's important is not necessarily to *be* funny, but rather to allow yourself to *see* the funny in a stressful or challenging situation. Or, at least, to allow yourself to momentarily step away from a stressful situation and find the humor in other aspects of your life. This is a habit that anyone can master.

The more you challenge yourself to see the humor during adverse times, the more you will be able to bounce back, get the job done and enjoy your life. Seeing the humor during challenging times is an indispensable tool to help you bounce back and stay motivated.

Here's something that can help. When you become aware that your emotions are veering out of control, stop, take a deep breath and ask yourself any number for the following warning questions:

"What will be the consequences if I hold on to this anger?"

"I have an important meeting with a client. Am I putting my best foot forward now?"

"What will happen if I don't get my shift together?"

"I have an extremely busy day. Am I in the mood I need to be in to get things done?"

"Are my fears keeping me from succeeding?"

"What can I do to turn this mood around?"

"What would Steve Rizzo say if he could see me now?" (Or substitute *"my mother"* for *"Steve Rizzo."*)

These types of questions act like radar, warning you that you're spinning out of control and becoming dangerously negative. More importantly, warning questions are good reminders that there are better ways to deal with frustrating and chaotic events than clinging to worst-case scenarios. Again, it's impossible to stay motivated when it seems that your world is spinning out of control.

Here is one humorous strategy to get you on your way. The next time you're at the breaking point of losing it, imagine that your inner voice is taking on the role of a news reporter giving you the blow-by-blow account of what is happening inside you.

"We interrupt your regularly scheduled life to bring you this special news bulletin! This is a message from your emotional broadcasting system. It has been brought to our attention that you are late, stuck in traffic, and your back sweat is turning your seat into the Everglades! You are now being tested to evaluate the severity of the negative situation. Right now you have a choice! You can either laugh, learn the lesson life is trying to teach you, move on with confidence and enjoy the day, and get motivated, or you can suffer from inner conflict, get angry, lose control and let opportunities pass you by! Back to you in the studio, Chuck."

Truly successful people attempt to understand the mystery and drama in life, but they also give their Humor Beings freedom to explore and acknowledge life's hilarities, absurdities and incomprehensibilities at the same time. It is the combination of the two points of view that leads to a healthy existence.

Common Sense Success Strategy

Unleash the power of your Humor Being on a daily basis. Take time out every day to find the laughter within you and all around you. It's there. Trust me. Better yet, trust yourself. You may have to look hard to find it or even create it out of thin air. The easiest way to do this is to make fun of your own frustration. Take a moment to get outside of yourself and watch what happens.

Remember, what's important is not to necessarily be funny in a stressful situation, but rather to see the funny in a stressful situation. Or to allow yourself to temporarily step away from stressful moments and seek the laughter in other aspects of your life. That's the real shift.

— STRATEGY 4 —

IGNITE YOUR PASSION & ENTHUSIASM

Now that you've made the choice to start your day in a good mood with a little laughter and kick-ass attitude, the next step to get motivated is to declare to yourself and the entire universe that you are going to enjoy the day. Once again, this is not pie-in-the-sky optimism. Spoken daily, words of encouragement, hope and joy are seeds that will always bear soul-nourishing fruit. Conversely, fruit from words that signify inadequacy, chaos and hopelessness will no doubt give your soul, well, at the very least, indigestion. So, instead of complaining about the way things are going to be, declare how you want them to be.

As soon as you've acquired an attitude of gratitude and are in a State of Feeling Good, get out of bed, plant your feet on the ground and say (preferably out loud, depending on who is still sleeping), "I'm going to enjoy this day!" Say it with conviction. Turn your Humor Being loose!

"I'm going to enjoy this day!"

Say it as you are taking a shower and as you are getting dressed. Announce it to your toaster, iPhone or computer.

"Good morning, toaster! Good morning, iPhone! And good morning to you, computer! Did you know that I'm going to enjoy this day?"

If they answer back, seek help immediately.

Say it to your entire family as you're eating breakfast. But please, make sure you've chewed your food. There's no need to be disgusting.

"I'm going to enjoy this day!"

Every now and then, throw in "Happiness and a State of Feeling Good is my number one priority today!" I also suggest an occasional affirmation—my favorite: "Whatever this day brings, there's that in me that is strong enough to meet it, learn from it and be blessed by it." Continue to put your attention on the things that make you feel good. If you get your words and attitude going in the right direction, you'll see a shift in the way your day and life are going.

As you are reciting your affirmations and proclaiming your joy to the world, there's something else you can add: imagine yourself enjoying and even laughing during the activities of the coming day. Visualization is a very important tool that can help you stay motivated. The key to making visualization effective is to have fun with it and do it with passion and enthusiasm. See and feel the excitement of your day as it unfolds. Include every detail. See yourself succeeding in all of your business endeavors.

For example, if you have an important meeting to attend or a proposal to make, envision yourself feeling confident and energized. Imagine yourself having fun with coworkers, associates or whomever is involved. Visualize yourself being congratulated.

If you're a nurse, see yourself laughing with your patients and their families and as you interact with your coworkers. If you are a teacher, envision yourself connecting with your students.

If traffic is always a problem on your commute, plan ahead and imagine yourself being calm (a favorite of mine). Know that you can't control the traffic, but you can control your emotions. For an extra boost, have your favorite music, audio books, motivational programs or comedians available for your listening pleasure. Visualize yourself singing or laughing behind the wheel as everyone else gets angry, bored and frustrated.

Visualizing how you want your day to go instills faith along with increased desire and intention that will empower you. Then, when something wonderful happens—or you find yourself actually enjoying the day and the people you come into contact with—the whole cycle will be reinforced, negative emotions will be easier to fend off and, most likely, choose to stay in bed.

The point is that you want to start your day off with high energy and a positive attitude. Too many people begin in a bad or low mood at best. What makes it worse is that they have no idea why. That is to say, people may not be conscious of the fact that they are focusing on what is broken instead of what can be created. As soon as they open their eyes, they go over their problems and think about—even visualize—the chaos from the day before and the grueling day that lies ahead. If only they understood that they can choose alternatives that will help them stay motivated. Because they may be so caught up in the insanity of their current situation, there is no room in their head for healthier or more productive thoughts. If only they would switch their focus, they could at least get some relief from the bombardment of negativity that assaults their morning ritual.

The greatest benefit of genuinely enjoying the day is that you generate a massive amount of positive energy.

But, now that *you* have established a positive morning routine, don't think you're off the hook and that later on you can go back to your old way of thinking. Keep the motivation going. Maintain your attitude of gratitude throughout the day.

For example, let's say you're driving through or flying over some beautiful landscape that touches you in some way. Don't let the feeling pass. Hold onto it. Savor it. Let yourself feel the wonder of it and allow your heart to soar. If you witness an act of kindness that puts a smile on your face, hold onto that as a reminder of how wonderful people can be and do something at least as kind in the next twenty-four hours. If someone says, "Have a nice day," don't just let it slide. Acknowledge the person and say, "Hey, don't tell me what to do! This is going to be a crappy day, and your telling me to have a nice one just made it worse." I'm obviously having some fun here. A better response might be "You know what? I will have a nice day. Thanks. You do the same."

The greatest benefit of genuinely enjoying the day is that you generate a massive amount of positive energy. It's manifested in passion and enthusiasm, and both are very contagious. Put another way, enjoyment is the spark that ignites passion and enthusiasm. Read that again and remember it. C'mon, I said read it again! Thank you.

I'm not claiming that by making a commitment to enjoy the day you won't be confronted by challenges. Of course you will! There will always be obstacles of some kind to overcome. True, there will be times when chaos and negative forces surround you, but you don't have to let them inside. It may not be easy at first, but as you condition yourself to prepare for the day ahead with gratitude, joyful statements and positive visualization, you will notice that stressful outside forces don't bother you as much. Ultimately, what you are doing is creating the ability to bounce back, and that's an all-important life skill.

It comes down to this: the unexpected is waiting for you. Countless outside factors can make or ruin your day, many of which are not in your direct control. So, it makes sense to seize control of what you can. Whether you're in an up or down period, remind yourself that feeling good and true happiness (and inner peace) are your number one priority. Even one situation a day in which you are able to invoke your grateful feelings and choose to be happy in the moment can have a tremendous impact on your life. I don't mean to suggest that you become the Dalai Lama, but if you do, please smile and bless the rest of us.

One last point (I promise) is the necessity to take action with passion and enthusiasm instead of just going through the motions. It's crucial to staying highly motivated.

When times are tough, passion and enthusiasm push you to go that extra mile. They propel you into a zone where you feel confident, courageous and victorious. Failure is not an option and every mistake is viewed as a do-over. When something doesn't turn out the way you planned, you don't even consider defeat. You're in such a high state of mind that you'll find yourself saying, "Okay, that didn't work. What do I have to do to turn this around? Who can I go to for help?" and "I know I can do this!"

Common Sense Success Strategy

Practice shifting into a State of Feeling Good. Get out of bed, plant your feet on the ground and declare to the entire universe, "I'm going to enjoy this day!" and "I choose to be happy now!" Say it as you are taking a shower and getting dressed. Allow yourself to let go and have a BLAST with this!

Focus on what's working in your life and what you're grateful for. Don't fixate on everything that has to be done; rather, think about who you have to be in order to get it done.

Occasionally recite your favorite affirmation. Visualize yourself enjoying, laughing and succeeding during activities of the coming day.

Remember: If feeling good is the fuel that drives motivation, then enjoyment shifts motivation into high gear.

Notice how much better you feel as you're starting your day and keep that attitude going throughout.

— STRATEGY 5 —

VISUALIZE & IT WILL MATERIALIZE

Another powerful strategy that can keep you motivated is the art of visualization. I know I touched upon this earlier, but this strategy is definitely worth mentioning in more detail. As I've often said, "Visualize and it will materialize."

Visualization is the application of your given gift of imagination to your faith and confidence. You can use it to discover ways to work through tough times, rise above your problems and see the possibilities of a solution. It can also be used in the process of healing or to manifest a particular desire.

Doubt can be the great nullifier when you want something. When I visualize what I'm asking for as being answered, I am more confident, and my results are enhanced. Having an unshakable belief that my desires will manifest at the right time is certainly empowering. But seeing what I want in full detail reinforces the positive feelings I need to stay motivated throughout the day, regardless of setbacks and challenging circumstances. That continual motivation and the feelings that fuel it are crucial.

As you visualize, crank up your energy. I mean, really get into this! It won't have much of an effect if you're casually looking at yourself in the picture. You must *enthusiastically be in* the picture as if it's really happening. Feel the excitement. Include every detail. Feel and experience the emotions as if you already have what you want.

If your desire is to create a meaningful relationship, you might want to picture the two of you laughing or holding hands walking on a beach. Perhaps you can envision having dinner together at a cozy romantic restaurant and sharing a meaningful conversation. The point is to feel the excitement of already having the relationship you want. For a little extra oomph, give thanks for the outcome you desire and know that it might take a while, but somehow, some way, you will eventually meet the right person.

It doesn't end there. Continue visualizing your desire with passion and enthusiasm throughout the day. This keeps negative emotions such as fear of failure, doubt and uncertainty from interfering. Also, know that you have to take action. In other words, you can't have a meaningful conversation at a cozy restaurant unless you are motivated enough to set the date, time and make a reservation. Remember what Einstein said, "Nothing happens unless something moves." Rizzo says, "Your life won't happen unless you move." So move! Do your part! Take action! Get motivated! Stay motivated! And don't give up!

When I made the decision to shift careers from standup comedian to motivational speaker, I didn't expect to wake up the next morning and say, "Okay, when do I speak?" That's ridiculous, of course. I was well aware that action needed to be taken. I knew I had to reinforce my foundation of faith and confidence. There was a well thought-out, step-by-step process involved.

Here's the thing, dear reader. At various times throughout the day, during the process of creating my new career, I visualized myself on stage speaking to thousands of people. I envisioned the audience laughing at my jokes and funny stories and acknowledging my message. I saw myself getting standing ovations and people thanking me for giving them hope. I envisioned agencies and clients from all venues calling my office wanting to book Steve Rizzo. I saw my calendar being filled with speaking engagements. I envisioned my fees and product sales increasing. I saw my team and agents calling me and saying, "You have another firm offer!" It took time and a great deal of dedication before I started reaping the benefits of my labor, but I did eventually get the things that I envisioned. And it's still paying off.

Common Sense Success Strategy

Take a few moments every day—throughout the day—to visualize the things you desire. Feel them with your heart and soul. See them in your mind as if they're really happening. Include every detail. Feel and experience the emotions as if you already have what you want.

— STRATEGY 6 —

MEDITATION & THE MOTIVATION FACTOR

Meditation is a very powerful activity that connects you to a higher part of yourself. People sometimes ask me why I meditate. I simply say, "It manages my mind and, believe me, that's a lot of managing." Meditation makes me feel safe and confident. I don't meditate every day. When I don't, the hectic world will usually have its way with me.

There are many different types of meditation techniques, but the main goal is to train your mind so you can become aware and at peace in your surroundings. For a lot of people, meditation is very challenging. That's because it's difficult to sit still and quiet the mind. As with anything in life, however, the more you practice, the easier it becomes. I'm not going to fill the next few pages with information on how to meditate or what techniques to practice. Others are more qualified on this subject. The Internet and bookstores are filled with how-to information and the associated benefits. I do urge you to make meditation a part of your daily life.

My only purpose for discussing this is to show you how this wonderful activity has transformed my life with hardly any effort at all. Throughout the years, various meditation techniques have given me clarity over challenging circumstances, guided me to make the right choices, revealed solutions to major problems and taken me from states of hopelessness to total inner peace and awareness. In short, no matter what is transpiring within me or around me, meditation ALWAYS, ALWAYS, ALWAYS makes me feel good. As you well know by now…feeling good is the fuel that drives motivation!

The following story is an example of how meditation revealed a solution to a problem and gave me the confidence to get motivated in the right direction.

A Leap of Faith

At the beginning stages of my speaking career, I was still performing as a comedian in clubs and theaters throughout the country. Comedy was, by far, my main source of income. Then, an unexpected problem arose. My comedy bookings were interfering with my speaking schedule. Every time the agency that booked my speaking engagements had a client that was interested in my services, the agent had to check my calendar to see if I was booked at a comedy club or theater. More often than not, I was, which meant they had to say no to the client.

One day, the President of the agency voiced her opinion. She made it quite clear that my current situation had become counterproductive and that she understood my financial concerns, but if speaking was my career of choice, I had to drop the comedy bookings and trust that speaking engagements would come in abundance.

I knew she was right, and I knew a decision had to be made, but to be honest, I was afraid to make it. I was pouring a lot of money into my speaking business and had recently purchased a house that was being renovated. "What if the money doesn't come in?" I thought. "What if I can't pay the bills?" "What if I can't pay the mortgage?" "What if..." Yes, that's right. Old fears and negative beliefs that I thought I had under control were coming back to haunt me with a vengeance.

One morning, during meditation, a scene from an Indiana Jones movie kept running through my mind. *The Last Crusade* starring Harrison Ford and Sean Connery. "Great," I thought, "I'm trying to clear my mind and I get a movie." Because I have always been involved in the wonderful world of show business, images, visions and dreams often occur in the guise of actors, musicians and such. It is what's closest to my heart. My soul knows this, so it relates to me this way.

Knowing not to disregard images or messages of any kind, I enthusiastically began to interpret its significance. Here's the setup:

Indiana's father is dying from a gunshot wound, and the only thing that can save him is the healing power of the Holy Grail. To acquire it, Indy has to go through a series of life-threatening tasks. In a race against time, he finally comes to the edge of a canyon and is faced with the last and most dangerous task of all: the test of Faith. The Grail is on the other side. Indy must make a leap of faith and step off the edge and know that he will not fall to his death. Somehow, some way, something will support him and keep him from falling into the abyss.

Time is of the essence. Indy holds his breath, looks down, puts his hand over his heart, says a silent prayer and takes his first step into the nothingness. He is in awe when he discovers that he didn't fall to his death. Instead, he's supported by a foundation—a transparent pathway that guides him to the other side. He passed the test of Faith.

Taking that first step is the vision I saw over and over again during my meditation. It was obvious to me what needed to be done. I needed to take a leap of faith of my own, knowing that I wouldn't fall. That very day, I decided not to accept any more comedy bookings. I was determined to follow my heart and put all of my energy, faith and motivation into my speaking career. The results have been staggering!

I sometimes wonder what would have happened had I allowed fear to keep me from making that leap.

Common Sense
Success Strategy

Take a few moments throughout the day to quiet and manage your mind through meditation. Notice how much better you feel and how you become empowered.

— STRATEGY 7 —

THE MARK OF
A TRUE LEADER

The most important lesson that I've learned from living on this planet is what any truly successful, happy and optimistic person knows about life:

They will experience good times and bad.

They will have sad days and ecstatic moments.

Nothing in life is permanent, and our success and happiness depend on our ability to ride these waves of change with equanimity.

Happy, successful and optimistic people are not exempt from trials and tribulations. In fact, many of them have to overcome unbelievably difficult circumstances to get to where they are today. What they all have in common, though, is their uncanny ability to shift their focus to a higher part of themselves.

They allow themselves to temporarily step away from those moments that are bringing them down or causing them pain and immediately focus on aspects of their lives that bring them joy and lift their spirits. They feel grateful for the things life has given them rather than cursing the unwanted things or what they've been denied.

I admire the way they find the laughter during tough times and sometimes even during the worst. It's not a question of putting blinders on and ignoring that they are going through difficulty, but rather that they instinctively know when to shift their mindset to something that will help them stay optimistic and, in turn, put them on a more productive path. In reality, we all have the power to do this. It's called a Power Shift in Focus.

Being able to create a Power Shift in Focus is one habit that can have a tremendous impact on your life. Why? Because it's a direct answer to the question life is always asking of you: "Who do you think you are?" When you temporarily step away from challenging situations and steer your attention to something that makes you feel good, you are thereby replenishing your spirit and nourishing your soul, the very essence of who you are. You are recharging your inner battery with the emotional fortitude needed to forge ahead. When you do go back to face a tough situation—which, by the way, is inevitable—you will feel less overwhelmed and the answers will come to you more readily. This is because you've calmed your nervous system down to the point where you can embrace the situation rather than have it control you. You don't have to be a rocket scientist to figure out that this shift in thinking is the mark of a true leader and can turn you into a real Motivated Shift Head.

You can always choose to shift to a positive state of mind when unwanted things happen.

You can't stop life from throwing stuff at you. You can't stop the unexpected from interfering with your goals and dreams. You cannot stop change from taking place. But you can always choose how to respond. You can always choose to shift to a positive state of mind when unwanted things happen. People who are happy, successful and optimistic know that, no matter what happens, life still goes on and they can choose to focus on things that empower them. They refuse to give up their right to succeed and enjoy life. And guess what? So can you.

A Power Shift in Focus, even if only for a very few moments, can have a profound effect on how you cope with any challenge and help you understand the great duality of life. In other words, you can't know true peace until you've experienced chaos. You can't know joy unless you've felt pain. Conversely, no matter how many tears may fall, there is still room for a smile—even laughter. You must experience one end of the emotional spectrum to fully appreciate the other. A Power Shift in Focus is a skill that nourishes your soul and significantly changes how you view life. It can be improved with practice and is a key to success and happiness.

Common Sense
Success Strategy

Temporarily step away from those moments that are bringing you down and focus on aspects of yourself that lift you up. Be grateful for the things that life has given you rather than cursing what you are lacking. And always find the laughter during tough times. This is what happy, successful and optimistic people know.

A Power Shift in Focus, even if only for a few moments, can have a profound effect on how you cope with any challenge and help you understand the great duality of life.

The Choice Is Yours

No matter what your current circumstances, feeling good and being happy should be your number one priority. When you become aware of this fact and incorporate the Common Sense Success Strategies offered in this book, you will be truly amazed at the many positive effects you'll experience.

Remember, only you can make yourself feel good. Seize opportunities to do so, and you will see a huge difference in how motivated you are and in how your daily life unfolds.

We constantly find ourselves in serious situations that can make us feel miserable, drain our joy and undermine the feeling that we deserve happiness now. Despite the burden these situations can have on our body, mind and spirit, and despite the intense moments of fear, self-doubt, guilt, anger and many other negative emotions, it is all part of the human experience. The big question is, to what extent will you allow these negative emotions to consume you? Will you let them dictate the choices you make and the actions you take? Will you allow them to regulate the degree of your overall happiness (which, in turn, will regulate your motivation level)? Don't be a victim of your emotions.

If you make the grave mistake of allowing your circumstances to dictate the degree of your overall happiness, you run the risk of missing out on the joy and success life has to offer.

I'm well aware that people operate on different clocks, but it's imperative that you allow yourself to rebound from challenging situations and pay attention to the aspects of your life that lift you up and empower you. Life goes on regardless of what happens to you or around you, so why not make the best of it? This is something successful, happy and optimistic people know. This is what keeps them motivated. The good news is that you have a choice. This, too, is part of being human.

When happiness and a State of Feeling Good become a habit, you will be able to stay motivated and weather the storms of chaos and misfortune with the knowledge that although your circumstances may not be ideal, your attitude is.

The longer you remain unhappy, the greater the opportunity for negative emotions to control your state of mind. If you make the grave mistake of allowing your circumstances to dictate the degree of your overall happiness, you run the risk of missing out on the joy and success life has to offer.

Remember: The more you concentrate on what you lack, the more of it you will get back. The more you focus on what is failing, the more your life won't work.

Remember: The more you focus on what is working in your life, the more you appreciate what you have, the more you elevate your degree of overall happiness. That is singularly the most important lesson I've learned, and I learned it the hard way. In fact, I learned most things the hard way. (Especially when asked, "Does this make me look fat?" There is no right answer to this question, so don't fall into the trap. Just shake your head emphatically and back away slowly.) And *that* is why I wrote this book. I hope it will make your life a little easier.

Remember: Your Humor Being is of your higher self. It's the part of you that brings out the best in you when times are tough. Acknowledge its power at all times. And please, don't forget to laugh throughout the course of a day. When it seems your world is falling apart and powerful, when negative emotions are closing in on you, muster up